THANKS BE TO GOD

Prayers from around the world

Selected and illustrated by
Pauline Baynes

Lutterworth Press
Cambridge

With gratitude for Fritz

Lutterworth Press
P.O. Box 60
Cambridge CB1 2NT

British Library Cataloguing in Publication Data

Thanks be to God.
1. Children. Christian life. Prayers – devotional works
242' .. 82

ISBN 0-7188-2781-3

Printed in Belgium

Dear God, be good to me, the sea is so wide
and my boat is so small.

Prayer of the Breton Fishermen

God of all our cities,
Each alley, street and square,
Pray look down on every house,
And bless the people there.

Joan Gale Thomas

God bless the field and bless the furrow,
Stream and branch and rabbit burrow,
Hill and stone and flower and tree,
From Bristol town to Wetherby –
Bless the sun and bless the sleet,
Bless the lane and bless the street,
Bless the night and bless the day,
From Somerset and all the way
To the meadows of Cathay;
Bless the minnow, bless the whale,
Bless the rainbow and the hail,
Bless the nest and bless the leaf,
Bless the righteous and the thief,
Bless the wing and bless the fin,
Bless the air I travel in,
Bless the mill and bless the mouse,
Bless the miller's bricken house,
Bless the earth and bless the sea,
GOD BLESS YOU AND GOD BLESS ME.

Prayer from England

For rosy apples, juicy plums,
And yellow pears so sweet,
For hips and haws on bush and hedge,
And flowers at our feet,
For ears of corn all ripe and dry,
And coloured leaves on trees,
We thank you, Heavenly Father God,
For such good gifts as these.

Prayer from England

All good gifts around us
Are sent from heaven above;
Then thank the Lord, O thank the Lord,
For all his love.

Matthias Claudius (1740-1815)

Thank you, God, for this sunny morning,
it makes me happy.

A child's prayer from England

May my mouth praise the love of God this morning.
O God, may I do your will this day.
May my ears hear the words of God and obey them.
O God, may I do your will this day.
May my feet follow the footsteps of God this day.
O God, may I do your will this day.

Prayer from Japan

God our Father, Creator of the world,
please help us to love one another.
Make nations friendly with other nations;
make all of us love one another like brothers.
Help us to do our part to bring peace in the
world and happiness to all men.

Prayer from Japan

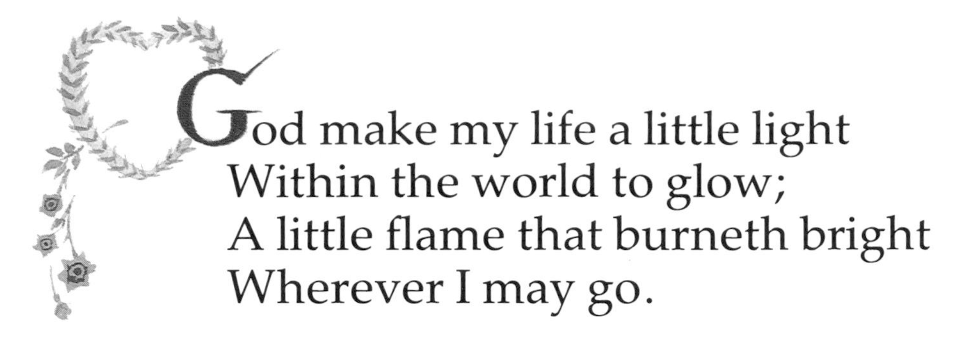

God make my life a little light
Within the world to glow;
A little flame that burneth bright
Wherever I may go.

Matilda Barbara Betham-Edwards (1836-1919)

God bless all those that I love;
God bless all those that love me.
God bless all those that love those that I love
And all those that love those that love me.

From an old New England sampler

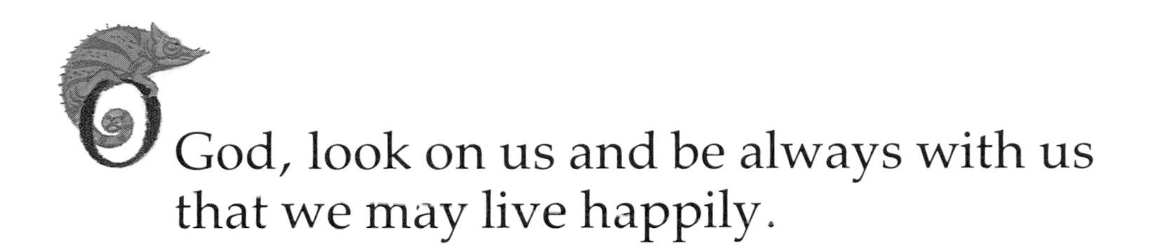

O God, look on us and be always with us
that we may live happily.

Prayer of the Amazulu people

Oh thou great Chief,
light a candle in my heart,
that I may see what is therein,
and sweep the rubbish from thy dwelling place.

Prayer of an African schoolgirl

O God who created and loves all creatures,
I think of the animals that must work so hard,
the oxen that have to pull heavy burdens,
and the donkeys that carry big loads.

Care for the hungry donkeys
and make people kind to animals.

A child's prayer from India

Dear Father, hear and bless
Thy beasts and singing birds,
And guard with tenderness
Small things that have no words.

Prayer from England

From ghoulies and ghosties and long-leggety beasties
And things that go bump in the night,
Good Lord, deliver us!

Prayer from Scotland

O God, my Guardian, stay always with me.
In the morning, in the evening,
by day, or by night, always be my helper.

Prayer from Poland

Forgive me, Lord, for thy dear son,
The ill that I this day have done,
That with the world, myself and thee,
I, ere I sleep, at peace may be.

Thomas Ken, Bishop (1637-1711)

As the daylight follows night,
As the stars and moon give light,
So, dear Lord, with all your might,
Care for me.

As the Springtime brings the flowers,
As the minutes turn to hours,
So, dear Lord, with all your powers,
Care for me.

As with Peace the swift-winged Dove,
Looks upon me from above.
So, dear Father, with thy love,
Care for me.

Olwen T. Godwin

For this new morning with its light,
Father, we thank Thee;
For rest and shelter of the night,
Father, we thank Thee;
For health and food, for love and friends,
For everything Thy goodness sends,
Father in heaven, we thank Thee.

Ralph Waldo Emerson

Thank you, God, for this new day
In my school to work and play.
Please be with me all day long,
In every story, game and song.
May all the happy things we do
Make you, our Father, happy too.

A child's prayer from England

Thank you for the world so sweet
Thank you for the food we eat,
Thank you for the birds that sing,
Thank you, God, for everything.

Mrs. E. Rutter Leatham

Let us with a gladsome mind
Praise the Lord for he is kind;
For his mercies shall endure
Ever faithful, ever sure.

John Milton (1608-1694)

I thank you Lord, for knowing me
better than I know myself,
And for letting me know myself
better than others know me.
Make me, I ask you then,
better than others know me.
Make me, I ask you then,
better than they suppose,
And forgive me for what they do not know.

A Muslim prayer

My father, all last year you took care of me and now you have given me a birthday. I thank you for all your goodness and kindness to me. You have given me loving parents, a home, gifts and clothes. Thank you, God. Help me to be a better child in my new year, to grow strong, to study well, to work happily.

Prayer from India

Lord, make me an instrument of thy peace,
Where there is hatred, let me sow love,
Where there is injury, pardon,
Where there is discord, union,
Where there is doubt, faith,
Where there is despair, hope,
Where there is darkness, light,
Where there is sadness, joy.

Francis of Assisi (1182-1226)

Thank God for rain
and the beautiful rainbow colours
and thank God for letting children
splash in the puddles.

A child's prayer from England

Teach me, my God and King,
In all things Thee to see,
That what I do in anything
To do it unto Thee.

George Herbert (1593-1632)

O most merciful redeemer,
Friend and brother,
May we know Thee more clearly,
Love Thee more dearly,
And follow Thee more nearly,
Now and ever.

Richard of Chichester (1197-1233)

O Father of goodness,
We thank you each one
For happiness, healthiness,
Friendship and fun,
For good things we think of
And good things we do,
And all that is beautiful,
Loving and true.

Prayer from France

Dear Lord, teach me to be generous;
To give and not to count the cost,
To work and not to seek for any reward,
Save that of knowing that I do your will.

Ignatius Loyola (1491–1556)

Dear Father of us all, we thank you for all the happiness of every day. We thank you for all the good things you give to us.
Help us to make other people happy too.

A child's prayer from England

God be in my head and in my understanding;
God be in mine eyes and in my looking;
God be in my mouth and in my speaking;
God be in my heart and in my thinking;
God be at my end and at my departing.

Sarum Primer (1527)

Blessed are you, Lord our God,
King of the universe, who has withheld nothing
from your world; and has created therein
beautiful creatures and goodly trees
for the enjoyment of mankind.

A traditional Hebrew prayer

You, O God, sustain all, do good to all, and provide food for all the creatures you have created. Blessed are you, O Lord, who sustains all.

A traditional Hebrew prayer

Our Father, who art in heaven,
Hallowed be thy name.
Thy kingdom come,
Thy will be done,
   On earth, as it is in heaven.
Give us this day our daily bread
And forgive us our trespasses,
   As we forgive those who trespass against us.
And lead us not into temptation,
   But deliver us from evil.
For thine is the kingdom,
The power and the glory,
For ever and ever,
Amen.

The Lord's Prayer

Acknowledgements

We would like to thank all the publishers and authors who have kindly given us permission to include their prayers in this book, as indicated in the list below.

Cassell plc: "God of all our cities," by Joan Gale Thomas from *God Of All Things,* (Mowbray and Co.) "Thank you God for this new day," "Thank you God for rain," "Dear Father of us all, we thank you" and "Thank you God for this sunny morning," from *The Infant Teacher's Prayer Book.* (Blandford Press.) Mrs Elizabeth Fisher: "O Father of goodness," A Prayer from France from *An Anthology of Prayers* by A S T Fisher, Longman Group Ltd. Lion Publishing plc: "May my mouth praise the love of God," A Prayer from Japan, and "O God, my guardian, stay always with me," A Prayer from Poland, from *The Lion Book of Children's Prayers,* 1977. The National Society: "Thank you for the world so sweet," © E Rutter Leatham, from *Hymns and Songs for Children,* National Society, 1964. New Century Publishers Inc: "O God who created and loves all creatures," A Children's Prayer from India, "God our Father, Creator of the World," A Prayer from Japan, and "My Father, all last year you took care of me and now", A Prayer from India from *Children's Prayers From Other Lands* by Gladys Spicer Fraser © 1954. Simon and Schuster International Group: "I thank you God for knowing me," A Muslim Prayer from *Book of Prayers* compiled by Helen Slater and illustrated by Adrian Moore, A Purnell Book published by MacDonald and Co. W I Books Ltd: "As the Daylight Follows Night," by Olwen T Godwin and "For rosy apples, juicy plums," from *A Book of Childhood Prayers and Verses* compiled by Carolyn Martin, Hodder and Stoughton Ltd.

Every effort has been made to trace and contact copyright owners. If there are any inadvertent omissions in the acknowledgements we apologise to those concerned and will be pleased to make any necessary corrections in future printings.

Where authors' dates are not given it is our belief they are alive.